# A More Excellent Way

## The Way to Living An Abundant Life!

**James H. Mitchell**

Brother Hwan,
Pursue Excellence with a
Passion and it will lead you
TO "THE ABUNDANT LIFE"
[illegible signature]
2011

xulon
PRESS

Copyright © 2010 by James H. Mitchell

*A More Excellent Way*
*The Way to Living an Abundant Life*
by James H. Mitchell

Printed in the United States of America

ISBN 9781609577902

All rights reserved solely by the author. The author guarantees all contents are original and do not infringe upon the legal rights of any other person or work. No part of this book may be reproduced in any form without the permission of the author. The views expressed in this book are not necessarily those of the publisher.

Unless otherwise indicated, Bible quotations are taken from The Holy Bible, New International Version. Copyright © 1973, 1978, 1984 by International Bible Society. Used by permission of Zondervan; and The King James Version.

www.xulonpress.com

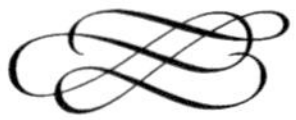

## *Special Thanks*

I agonized a bit over writing this paragraph, wanting to be profound yet clear, creative yet concise and not miss anyone. However, one of the many things I have learned about excellence during the journey of writing this book is: excellence demands we focus on the important elements in our life and strip away the excess. With that said, I would like to first thank my Lord and savior for His grace, patience and longsuffering for having to put up with all of the excuses (See Chapter 5 on procrastination) that occurred between: the writing of the first page and the last page of "A More Excellent Way". Secondly, I would like to say a special thank you to: my wife Krista, for all of the excellence she brings into the lives of her "Three Boys" (me and my 2 sons) everyday; my mother, who demonstrated excellence of heart and courage as she dealt with illness throughout her life and battled cancer without ever uttering a single complaint; to my father who has always chosen excellence over success throughout his ministry; and my editor (Brenda Pitts), who showed me through her excellent work, why I should stick to writing and leave the editing to the professionals. Lastly, but certainly not least, if your name does not appear in this limited space for special thanks and you believe that it should, please charge the oversight to my head and not my heart!

## *Dedication*

This book is dedicated to my sons Jeremiah and Julius. It is my sincere hope and daily prayer that when the last grains of sand fall out of dad's hour glass, you will have become peculiar men, who walk with Christ daily and have placed the pursuit of excellence far above the pursuit of success – men who have chosen a more excellent way!

# Contents

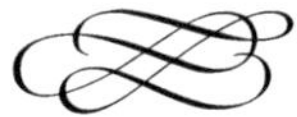

## Standing Eight Count

# An Introduction

If I just handed over some of my hard-earned cash and, more important, was about to invest some of my valuable time, for time as one writer put it "is the one immaterial object which we cannot influence—neither speed up nor slow down, add to nor diminish—it is an imponderably valuable gift" (Maya Angelo)- It would be nice to know what compelled the author to write the book I now hold in my hand?

So you want to know, what made me fill up yellow pad after yellow pad, stare into computer monitor after computer monitor, research source after source, pitch a myriad of agents and publishers in order to come up with this thing you now hold in your hand, this thing that takes all of the above and sums it all up with five letters—a book? That is a great question and I am glad you asked!

Well, it all started one morning while sitting at a desk—you know, the one positioned by the window with the great view of someone else sitting at an identical desk in an identical room across the courtyard. On this particular morning, I was preparing for a big presentation that offered the possibility of significant revenues for my company. And like so many of us do when we have something on the line, I thought it might be a good idea to make sure I had morning prayer and devotion. I began reading from the book of Ecclesiastes, trying to stay focused on the Word of God rather than the words of my presentation, which imposed on my devotion at will. I had no idea that a Scripture I must have read several times before would on this day change my life and my way of thinking forever.

Like an archaeologist seconds after a major discovery, I stood still with the revelation that the source from which I drew my principles for pursuing success, my philosophy on competition, and my motivation to win were at this moment being challenged by this new discovery, this tiny verse of Scripture. My years of playing intercollegiate football for one of the winningest coaches in NCAA history, my studies at one of the best business schools in the country, my sales training as a top sales rep for one of America's Fortune 500 companies, my experience as a CEO, and my work with hundreds of small-business owners and aspiring entrepreneurs now drew me into the fight of my life. My whole ideology for success was smack-dab in the middle of a standing eight count. For you boxing novices, a Standing Eight Count is given to a fighter who has been hit so hard that although he or she is still standing the fighter is stunned and totally defenseless.

After being hit with Ecclesiastes 4:4, my thoughts no longer drifted to my presentation; all my focus was on this tiny little verse, which I read over and over again in every translation I can get my hands on!

"I observed that the basic motivation for all success is envy and jealousy" (TLB).

"I have seen that every labor and every skill, which is done, is the result of rivalry between a man and his neighbor" (NASB).

"I saw that all labor and all achievement spring from man's envy of his neighbor" (NIV).

As I read each translation, I could hear the referee yelling at my ideas about real living and my philosophy of success: "Five . . . can you go on? Six ... how will you go about competing? Seven . . . Can you continue with business as usual?"

Was Solomon correct in implying that at the root of all of man's inspiration for achievement and success lie envy and jealousy? This can't be right in all cases; perhaps Solomon woke up on this particular morning without all of his wisdom. Does this mean God does not want us to be successful? How do we go about aspiring to achieve? How do we pursue success without envy and jealousy entering the picture? Is it impossible to want the best life has to offer without looking at our neighbors? And with every translation I read, it became painfully clear that I could not continue approaching life and pursuing success as usual, because from that moment forward, I would never see things the same way again. "EIGHT . . . (Old way of thinking), you're out!"

Have you ever wondered why your plans never seem to work out the way you envisioned, or why you have not been able to achieve the levels of success you envisioned for your life, your business, your marriage, your ministry, your relationships, your career, etc.? Why have the seeds that you planted not blossomed: that promotion that you get close to but never quite get your hands on, that recognition list you never find your name at the top of, those goals you set time and time again that you seem to always fall short of?

Have you ever uttered the words "Maybe God doesn't want this for me" or wondered why the things you've accomplished don't provide that feeling of satisfaction you envisioned they would bring? Didn't God tell us He would not withhold any good thing from us? So how come we don't have them yet? The answers to many of these questions will be found in this book, and every one of them will point one way—*a more excellent way!*

People are forgoing excellence in the pursuit of their dreams and in their quest for success. And the high cost of that oversight is true success. God may be keeping the whirlwinds of success from blowing in our lives simply because of our failure to follow heaven's recipe for success. The substitution of God's recommended ingredients may have cost many of us the true success we desire. **For many of us, it's not a lack of resources, desire, or effort; God may simply be holding back the whirlwinds of success purely because of our reasons for "being in the kitchen"; that is, why we want success.**

Some years ago (I use the word *some* so as not to date myself), there was a laundry-detergent commercial that showed the owner of a dry-cleaning business washing laundry with the advertiser's brand of detergent—a brand easily found on the shelves in any grocery store. A customer came into the store to pick up his laundered clothes and marveled at how clean and fresh the items were. The customer proceeded to ask the business owner, "How do you get my clothes so clean and fresh?" The store owner replied, "Ancient Chinese secret." When it comes to the pursuit of success, many of us are just like the customer in the laundry commercial; we look for the secret and follow all kinds of advice, techniques, programs, workshops, seminars, and infomercials in search of the road to success.

The book you are holding will reaffirm, just like the old laundry commercial, that there is no ancient Chinese secret when it comes to success. There are no shortcuts. There is only one way, and that way is the more excellent way that permeates the Word of God. Ecclesiastes 4:4 says that man's motivation to succeed is influenced by envy and jealousy of his neighbor. Therefore, if Solomon is right, then we need a more excellent way of approaching and pursuing success.

This book supplies answers, to many of the questions left unanswered by the popular prosperity theology of our time. *A More Excellent Way* explains the critical significance of Solomon's profound words for today's Christians and shares powerful, God-inspired revelations that will guide you to a more excellent way of living an abundant life; that is, identifying and pursuing true success.

**Discovering a more excellent way has changed my life forever. It has given me new insights on how to better resemble the peculiar person God has called each of us to be.** When it comes to success and competition, God is looking for a peculiar people with peculiar perspective, principles, and passion. God has given me the assurance that *A More Excellent Way* will liberate and empower those who read its pages. I am confident that you will receive immeasurable returns on your investment of time and money. May God bless you with each turned page!

## Chapter 1

# I'll Race You to the Corner!

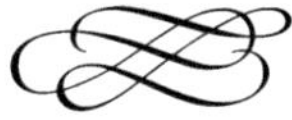

Have you ever yelled out, "I'll race you to the corner"? We can't help ourselves; the spirit to compete against our fellow man, to measure ourselves against the next guy or gal, is inherently a part of us. How many of us can recall as a youth, for no other reason than standing next to someone, blurting out, "Race you to the corner!" And depending on where we are from geographically, instead of the corner we may have cried, "Race you to the barn" or "to the flagpole" or "to the light pole." Even though we may not have uttered these exact words in quite some time, most of us still play the game of "race you to the corner."

However, these days we are not as forward with it, but it's still a big part of our psyche and day-to-day lives. Think about the last time you were at a traffic light and someone pulled up next to you with the same kind of car as yours. You didn't beep the horn and yell out to the person, "Hey, when the light turns green, I'll race you to the corner," but something inside you did say, "Race you to the corner! Ready or not, here we go!" Or maybe there's a new position in the office that is a big step up from where you are now, and you can hear the office halls echoing with the screams of "race you to the corner office!"

It's inherently a part of us—this burning desire to outdo, outperform, outrun, outearn, and outwit the other guy or gal. This desire is in us from birth and is then refined and reinforced throughout our lives. "Born in sin shapen in iniquity" - sound familiar? From childhood we are encouraged to be better than the other kid, the other sibling, the other relative, the other family, the other classmate, the other teammate. It should alarm us, but it doesn't, because we're constantly admonished to compete against our neighbor.

Consciously for some and subconsciously for others, many of us are consistently crying out, "Hey, neighbor! On your mark . . . get set . . . go! I'll race you to the promotion," "the cash," "the bank," "the net worth," "the new house," "the new car," or "the new job," we say. Solomon confirms that this is not a new phenomenon, for Ecclesiastes 4:4 let's us know that since the days of old we have been setting our sights on the guy next door, the girl in the next cubicle, the guy in the next church, the next pulpit, the next pew, the next city, the next state, the next country, the next race, the next color, the next creed, the next religion. No one cares how you run the race anymore; winning is paramount, and everything else is just a formality until a winner is decided. However, I submit to you that God is more concerned about the *journey* and less concerned about the *destination!*

God still does and forever shall care more about how you run the race and how you play the game! God still asks those forgotten questions: How did you get to the finish line? What did you sacrifice to get there? What was your motivation during the race? Were your tactics honorable, or did you sacrifice others along the way? Did you make any friends along the way? Men, women, girls, and boys have become so obsessed with winning that many today believe success and excellence are intertwined. However, no two things could be more distinctively different. **Success looks on the outward appearance, but excellence looks at the inward man—the spirit, heart, and soul of a man or woman.**

When we pursue success, what are we really pursuing? When we blurt out, "Race you to the corner!" whether in our spirits as adults or aloud as children, what are we really seeking? Many of us are looking for validation; we are seeking distinction from the status quo, affirmation that we are better, that our choices were the right choices. We want confirmation that we have something that others do not...what it takes to win! That's because all throughout our development, we have been conditioned to honor and praise "winners," the "successful" people, those folks who have made it to the top of their respective food chain; that is, the prettiest, the wealthiest, the strongest, the fastest . . . the list goes on and on. We have been conditioned to believe that those who possess the accoutrements of success are living the abundant life.

Think about it. In my earlier car example, you were looking at the guy next to you with the same car—the exact same make, model, year, color, and engine. Common sense would tell you that there is no difference between the two, yet something inside of you, after looking over and seeing somebody else driving "your car," insists on somehow proving that when your car came off the assembly line, it was better than all the others out there. And if the cars are identical, then you must make it clear that you have mastered the art of driving that particular model of car. And better yet, if the car is the same model, but a different year or make, the manufacturer now becomes the sponsor of your racing team, and you must prove that your year was "the year."

We want to win. No, scratch that—we must win! We must win because society has made it clear that winning is the only reason we should play the game. Society would have us believe that in the game of life, there are only two classes of people: winners and those who want to be winners (affectionately referred to as "losers" by the winners). But I submit that God still is more concerned about how we play the game than if we win gold, silver or bronze. **Man says, "Just win, baby! God says, "It's not all about winning; it's all about how you won and why you were able to win.**

A more excellent way mandates that how you play the game is just as important as winning the game. We all want to be winners; it's inherently a part of us. However, a more excellent way demands an honest answer to the following question: do I play the game in the spirit of true competition, striving to see where my preparation strategy and best efforts take me or do I play the game for the spoils of victory? Society has become more and more obsessed with the spoils than with the game itself, but God warns us of becoming obsessed with the spoils of victory. Do you remember a man named Achan in the book of Joshua? Achan became so obsessed with the spoils of victory that he lost sight of how God wanted His people to play the game. Achan lost sight of why he was playing the game and who he was playing for. Achan's actions adversely affected the entire team and destroyed his family. Pursuers of excellence are not obsessed with the spoils of victory; pursuers of excellence are focused on the process for victory!

A more excellent way causes us to take an inventory of the dynamics involved in the process rather than the dynamics surrounding victory. It's like the bumper sticker that reads, "He who dies with the most toys wins." That's a success-philosophy slogan, but if you think about it, it illustrates my point regarding focus. A subscriber to today's success theologies and philosophies will focus on the spoils of winning; in this case, the toys that financial success affords us: big homes, fast cars, big vacations, clothes, jewelry, status, prestige, etc. However, a person who subscribes to excellence will look at the process; in this case, life and death, and will see flaws in the slogan right away.

The first and most obvious flaw is... you have to die to win! Moreover, if you have to die in order to win, how do you ever get notified of your winnings; and if you have been living to acquire the most toys, when do you ever get enough time to enjoy them—especially if the game is over when you die? The Word of God tells us in Ecclesiastes 5:12 "the sleep of a laborer is sweet, whether he eats little or much, but the abundance of a rich man permits him no sleep." The rich man gets no sleep because he's too busy worrying about getting more or keeping what he has from others.

There is a game many of us played as a child, and some kids still play it today, called "king of the mountain." You know, it's the game where you find a mound of some sort or a small hill, and the first person to get to the top yells, "King of the mountain!" Then everyone else in the game goes after that person, seeking to gain what he or she has achieved—the spot at the top. When we as adults mentally yell, "I'll race you to the corner," it's like playing king of the mountain. If you analyze the game, you'll see the players are never at peace. While playing the game, they never have an opportunity to stand still long enough to enjoy their success because they are always doing one of two things: trying to get on top or trying to stay on top. Solomon, the wealthiest man in earth's history, writes, "As goods increase, so do those who consume them" (Eccles. 5:11, NIV). In other words, the more you have...the more people who show up wanting some of it. When you subscribe to today's success philosophy or popular prosperity theology, you are constantly pursuing success, because someone will always have more, or someone will always be bigger, stronger, or more popular.

A more excellent way forces us to place the process above the rewards. That's why God told us: "seek first the kingdom of God and all these things will be added onto you." God is admonishing us to focus on the process and when we do that the rewards will follow. When we focus on the process, we are forced to come to the realization that we have very little to do with the fact of standing in the winner's circle. We recognize that it was the impact of others on the process, particularly the hand of God that allowed us to achieve that which was necessary for us to realize our goals. When we focus on the process, we recognize the work and effort of the team.

It amazes me how so many "successful" people who finally begin to receive the things they felt would come along with their success turn around and divorce themselves from the very people who helped guide them through the process. Soon after they "arrive," some "successful" people divorce their spouses after years of depending on their help throughout the process. They choose instead to share the spoils of their success with people who contributed very little to the process that provided the success they now enjoy. This unfortunate common occurrence is the equivalent of rewarding only the new employees of a company for making the company the success it is today. When these kinds of events surround our successes, are we really winners, or merely losers who have stumbled into the winner's circle?

When we subscribe to a more excellent way, the words *I made it* will never be a part of our vocabulary because excellence is all about the process. And the word *process* dictates multiple variables working together to achieve a desired outcome. Therefore, a more excellent way mandates you adopt a *we* mentality, never an *I* mentality. With excellence, it's always *we* made it, *we* did it, *we* accomplished it, and more important, it reminds us that we were created by him (God) and for him (God)!

Deuteronomy 8:18 also galvanizes this aspect of a more excellent way: "But remember the LORD your God, for it is he who gives you the ability to produce wealth" (NIV). **When we subscribe to a more excellent way, the only permissible time we use the word *I* in describing our accomplishments is to say, "I could never have accomplished this without God and the help of others."**

Take a moment and think about some of your past or present successes, victories, and accomplishments. Then fill in the blanks below with the names of some of the people who helped you through the process:

________________________________________

________________________________________

________________________________________

________________________________________

________________________________________

Now, make sure you thank them again and again.

Growing up, I remember a television show called *The Six Million Dollar Man.* (Oh, I am giving my age away, aren't I?) The opening sequence for the show started out by saying, "We can make him better, stronger, and faster." I wonder what million-dollar man we would be up to today: the fifty-, seventy-five-, or hundred-million-dollar man? The billion-dollar man? It would never end, because man is never satisfied. Someone would have to make sure his or her man was the biggest, the strongest, and the fastest. **Winning at all costs has become everything, and we have all but forgotten a most valuable fact: *man honors those who achieve "success," but God honors those who pursue excellence!***

## Chapter 2

# It's Not a Rat Race—It's a Marathon

If you took a group of world-class sprinters and a group of world-class marathoners, placed them in a lineup, and then asked the average person to pick the team most likely to win a race, 99 percent of the time that team would be dominated by sprinters. This is because when comparing the appearance of sprinters with marathoners, sprinters are more physically striking. A world-class sprinter is very muscular and well defined and has a lot more mass than a world-class marathon runner. A marathoner is slender and lean, and standing next to an old defensive lineman like me, he or she might easily be called skinny. However, the question that most people fail to ask in this exercise is, what kind of race are the runners running?

I love the writings of the apostle Paul because Paul (like me) was a great sports enthusiast. Paul often used sports analogies to illuminate key points about the Christian journey. The term *Christian journey* is just a nickname for the word *life* used by people who have decided they want Christ to walk with them each and every day. When describing the Christian journey, Paul compares it to a race. Paul makes it distinctively clear that this race is not a hundred-meter dash, but a marathon. It is a race that will not be won by sprinters (the swift or the strong) looking for a speedy victory; rather, it will be won by runners who can go the distance. These are ordinary people determined to run until the end, runners who can overcome life's many difficult obstacles and challenges, runners who will persevere and run on, no matter what.

A lot can be learned about this journey of ours by looking at the significant differences between the two types of races. One of the major differences between a marathon and a sprint becomes clearly evident at the start of the race. In a sprint, you can see the finish line from the starting blocks, and you can focus your sights on the mark. However, at the start of a marathon, the finish line is nowhere in sight and will remain out of the line of sight for quite some time. This distinct difference forces marathoners to focus on the journey (the process of running the race) rather than the final destination (the finish line). A marathon forces the runners to master themselves. Marathoners must maximize their strengths, overcome their weaknesses, and demand that their bodies strive for excellence and deliver the best performance they possibly can.

However, the world's view of life's journey is quite different. The world likens this journey of ours to a different kind of race—a rat race! Many of today's success gurus will tell you to look to the finish line as your motivation to run. Take a picture of the things you want from success, and let those things inspire you to run, to fight, and to win, they say. But God says to look to Him and within yourself, and to keep pressing towards the mark, keep running towards the finish line. Man is obsessed with *winners,* but God is obsessed with *runners.*

Today's society is willing to win the rat race at any cost and is determined to succeed by any means necessary. But God has been and always shall be more concerned about those who are committed to finishing the race, not just winning it. That is why Paul uses the analogy of a marathon rather than an all-out sprint, because in a marathon, everyone who clocks in (crosses the finish line) is a winner. In a rat race, only those who come in at the top are considered winners. In a rat race, winning isn't everything—wining is the only thing!

Did you know that rats can never stop gnawing, scratching, and clawing? If a rat stops scratching and clawing, its claws will grow so long that its paws will be rendered useless. Additionally, if a rat stops gnawing, its teeth will become so long that they will grow straight through the bottom of its mouth. Therefore, those who subscribe to the rat race must constantly scratch, claw, and gnaw their way to the top. Once at the top, they must continue clawing, scratching, and gnawing until the day they die, never stopping to smell the roses and enjoy the fruit of their success.

Sprinters are constantly challenged; constantly defending their times; and constantly running qualifying races, quarterfinals, and finals. Then it starts all over again at the next competition. In a sprint, if the competitors do not win gold, silver, or bronze (first, second, or third), there is no place for them in the winner's circle. In life, God has given each of us different abilities, capabilities, talents, gifts, and resources, and God doesn't expect all of us to have the fastest time. One of the biblical examples of this is the parable of the three servants, more widely referred to as the parable of the talents.

Here you have a master who gave three servants resources (talents) to go out into the world (the race) and put those talents to work for him. The Bible says that "to one he gave five talents, to another two and to another one, to each according to their own ability…" (Matthew 25:15). The master distributed the talents to each servant according to his propensity to perform.

The master did not set this up as a race to see who would come in first, second, or third. His expectations for results directly correlated to the talents each servant was given to work with.

When I reported to football camp one summer, I learned that every player had to run a timed mile. The penalty for not meeting the predetermined mile time was to run a mile after practice every day until you met the expected time. The coaches knew that it would not be fair to set one time for the whole team because everyone's running ability was different. Thank goodness, linemen had their own time, because a big ole' defensive lineman like me was not equipped to run with the receivers, and running backs, no matter how hard I might try. On the other hand, when it came to the bench press, each position again had its own minimum requirement, because no matter how hard a wide receiver trained or tried, he was not going to be able to bench-press more than a big ole' defensive lineman like me.

God is the same way; He does not expect each of us to run the same race. However, God does expect each of us to take an honest survey of the blessings, gifts, and abilities He has given us and to keep striving for excellence until we reach the finish line. God expects us to "clock in." *Clocking in* is a term I use to express that God expects each of us to finish the race with a time that correlates to the gifts, talents, and resources He has equipped us with. To whom much is given, much is required. God expects us to reach within ourselves and run the best time we possibly can with what we have been given to work with – God expects us to compete in a more excellent way!

Does that mean that we except mediocrity? Absolutely not! It is just the opposite. **A more excellent way demands that each of us strive to do our very best within the framework of the blessings, gifts, and talents God has equipped us with.** When we choose a more excellent way, we are always in race against ourselves - always in pursuit of our personal best. We compete for the opportunity to achieve excellence. And if we consistently strive for excellence, we are guaranteed a place in the winner's circle! When we set out to parallel the success of others and set our sights on premeditated destinations, we are setting ourselves up for failure and disappointment.

There would not be a race without someone to run the second-, third-, and fourth-best times, and it would not be life if we all had been given the exact same gifts, talents, and abilities. When we take an inventory of our God-given blessings, gifts, talents, and abilities and set out to do our very best, we pave the way for victory and reward. Our victory is the accomplishment of excellence and the results of achieving excellence is success!

Remember the widow in Scripture who gave out of her poverty? Christ said her contribution was far greater than those who gave out of their abundance. She gave a more excellent gift, yet those who collected the money gave the credit to those who contributed the most. Sadly, our present society is saturated with runners who are looking for shortcuts, runners who are willing to skip the process and go straight to the winner's circle. They are willing to overlook character, overlook perseverance, overlook the process for excellence, and jump right to success. No wonder we have companies and executives like those at Enron, WorldCom, Lehman Brothers, AIG, Tyco, Bank of America, Morgan Stanley, and the list grows even as you read this book.

The obsession with success and winning has created a society of people who are more prone to lie about their successes than to share what they have learned by overcoming obstacles and challenges during the race. You may not clock in with the fastest time, the heaviest lift, the corner office, the largest church, the biggest home, the fastest car, the largest net worth, the greatest share of the market, the biggest profit, the most units sold, the mega church, the popular choir, the largest baptism, the greatest sermon, the most converts, the largest tithe, or the biggest offering; but when you make it about pursuing excellence with what God has given you, I guarantee that you will be victorious. I base my guarantee for success on the unequivocal fact that man rewards *winners,* but God rewards *finishers!*

One of the greatest dangers of today's success-and-prosperity theology is that it requires you to set your sights on predisposed destinations. One of the biggest dangers of such a myopic focus is that after such an intense pursuit of the destination, it's extremely difficult to move on once you arrive there. You may pick a destination that did not require you to give your best effort, utilize your God-given gifts, or showcase your talents. Arriving at that predetermined destination can cause you to miss the great successes God has planned for your future, because you now have what the Joneses have. However, when you continue to pursue excellence with the best God has given you, there is no limit as to what God can do or where He can take you. The Bible tells us that eyes have not seen, ears have not heard, neither has entered into the minds of men, the things God has in store for them that love Him. No wonder so many people are not satisfied with their lives, careers, relationships, business ventures, plans—their "success." **When we make it all about *success* rather than *excellence,* oftentimes we end up stuck in places God intended us to be for a moment.**

Therefore, if God has blessed you with the ability to be a doctor, don't stop with nursing.

If God has given you the talent to be a great attorney, don't settle at paralegal. If God has given you the ability to run a business, stop running someone else's and go start your own. If God has given you the resources to own a home, go find a realtor and stop paying someone else's mortgage. And if God has given you the intellect to get your PhD, don't stop at an AA. Moreover, if God has given you the spiritual gift of teaching, stop sitting in the back of the class and lead out in a Bible class or prayer meeting. If God has given you the gift of healing, stop reading the sick and shut-in list and go lay hands on somebody. If God has given you the gift of preaching, stop analyzing everyone else's sermons and go preach your trial sermon. If God has given you the gift of evangelism, stop spreading church gossip and start spreading the Good News. And if God has given you the spiritual gift of leadership, stop standing in the shadows and step forward, raise your hand, and cry out like Isaiah, "I'll go. Send me!"

A more excellent way helps us to more easily accept change and face new challenges. It reminds us that God is not standing at the finish line waiting for the first three runners to cross the line; God is waiting at the finish line with the same reward for everyone who crosses it. If you find yourself obsessed with success and winning at any cost, God has a more excellent way for you to accomplish your goals. In this marathon called life, you may not clock in with the fastest time, but when you make it about doing your best, with the best that God has equipped you with - I guarantee you will be victorious. Let men have their rat race and give their winners medals. Choose a more excellent way, and remember, God stands at the finish line waiting to give all who finish a crown!

## Chapter 3

# What Makes Your Motor Run?

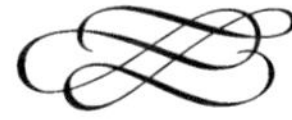

I have a nephew who came to live with us to participate in an internship after graduating from college. Like any good uncle would do, after showing him around the house, I showed him how to start the lawn mower, pointed out where the property line ended, and went out to enjoy a round of golf. When I returned some hours later, my nephew was still at it and was having some major problems finishing the job. When I asked him what had happened, he said that after he refueled the lawn mower, it started having problems. It would start, but then just when it was making progress, it would conk out. Then it began taking a long time to start back up, and so he wound up having to cut the lawn two feet at a time. I then proceeded to ask him to show me the gas can that he had used to refuel the lawn mower. When my nephew pointed to the smaller gas can, I instantly knew what the problem was: he had refueled the lawn mower with the wrong mixture of gas and oil.

For many of us, our pursuit of success is reminiscent of my nephew's lawn-mowing experience. We have put the wrong fuel mix into our success engines, and our pursuits of success have thus been one backfire after another—one long, disappointing journey. Motivation, however, is the fuel that powers our drive to succeed. If our fuel mix is wrong, then our success journey will be long, arduous, and, in some cases, completely unsuccessful.

When I speak on the topic of success and excellence, I make it a matter of practice to spend some time discussing a simple question: why do you want success? You would be surprised how many people go running to and fro in pursuit of success without ever really stopping to understand their reasons for going after it. And in the Christian community, we find many people embracing the success-and-prosperity theology of our time, running full speed ahead after success with no idea why they want it or, even more important, what they plan to do for God once they have it!

In Ecclesiastes 4:4, King Solomon says, "I observed that the basic motivation for all success is envy and jealousy" (TLB). That let's us know that man's motivation for success is greatly influenced (fueled) by external sources; that is, man's envy of his neighbor. Solomon is saying that as we see others and the benefits of their success, we become motivated to pursue the same things and our own success. We want those things we see around us, such as homes, cars, status, fame, fortune, big churches, large ministries, wealth, etc., and we believe they will bring us great satisfaction. Then we set out sights on a pursuit that will afford us those things. But let's assume you have been enlightened by the preceding chapters and no longer want success because of your neighbor's success. The question still remains, why do you want success?

What do you want to glean from it? What needs and desires do you want it to fulfill?

Take a moment, grab a pad (or use the space below), and write a list of all the reasons you want success. It's quite okay to put material things on this list, because we live in a world where material items are necessary for our existence.

Be sure to make your list before proceeding to the next section.

## Success Inventory List

1.
2.
3.
4.
5.
6.
7.
8.
9.
10

The Word of God says, "Commit to the LORD whatever you do, and your plans will succeed" (Prov. 16:3). Have you been praying to the Lord for many of the things on your list? Have you committed your plans for success to the Lord? Some of you have been praying for the things on your list every day, but nothing seems to have drastically changed in your life. Why haven't you received all of the success you have been praying for?

The text says, "Commit thy plans unto the Lord, and they will succeed." What does that really mean? When we commit to our spouses in marriage, we are essentially giving ourselves to each other, giving ourselves to the one we love. When we commit funds to a cause, we are giving those funds to those who advocate for the cause. When we commit our lives to Christ, we are giving ourselves to Him for His use and for His service. Therefore, when we commit our plans to the Lord, we are giving them to Him for His purpose, for His use, and for His glory. Although we may be praying about our plans and rightfully acknowledging that we need God's help to bring them to fruition, many of us have not truly committed them to the Lord. We have merely declared them before Him!

***Take a look at your list and think about how God will use those things you have written on it. What is the "God-plan" for each of them?***

I can see many of you scratching your heads. "A God-plan—what's that?" you say. If you have never used the term, don't feel guilty, because you are in good company. Solomon said that the whole duty of man (man's purpose) is to glorify God and keep His commandments (Eccles. 12:13–14). **A God-plan mandates that we ask ourselves a critical question: how will my success be used to glorify God and advance His kingdom?** This question is the litmus test for determining the right fuel mix; that is, our motivation for success.

The Word of God says, "Many are the plans in a man's heart, but it is the Lord's purpose that prevails" (Prov. 19:21). When it comes to our plans for success, there are two obstacles that many of us do not see. The first one is the fact that we are not committing our plans to the

Lord but are merely asking God to make them come true. The second is the fact that we have not attempted to line up our plans with God's purpose, but rather, we want God to incorporate our plans into His purpose. When we ask God to take His perfect will and A-line it with our imperfect will, it is the equivalent of trying to make oil and water one substance—it just won't work! And the reason it cannot work is that the text has a big ol' *but* in it. The text says, ". . . but it is the Lord's purpose that prevails." If our purpose in life is to serve God's purpose and advance His kingdom, then everything we pursue in life should have a God-plan associated with it.

Let's look at this dynamic in action. Remember Hannah, in the Old Testament? Hannah was unable to get pregnant for many years, and she prayed for a child so frequently and intensely that the temple priest thought she was a raving mad drunk (1 Sam. 1:12). What was the change that brought different results? Hannah modified her fuel mix (motivation) and incorporated a God-plan into her request. Hanna truly committed her plans to the Lord by aligning her purpose with God's purpose. After Hanna made the commitment to raise her son to be a servant of God, exactly nine months to the day of instituting her God-plan, she bore a son. And he was not just any son, but one whose life is documented in two books of the Bible that bear his name: 1 Samuel and 2 Samuel. Hanna chose a more excellent way!

Another awesome example of a more excellent way in action is the Solomon's response to God, when God told him he would grant him his heart's desire (1 Kings 3:5). When Solomon made his request known to God, rather than ask for the accoutrements of great power and success, Solomon asked for things to help him lead God's people and do God's will during his reign as king. As a result of Solomon's choosing a more excellent way and aligning his plans with God's purpose over his own, God not only granted Solomon's request but also rewarded Solomon with unprecedented wisdom and wealth. Solomon's fuel mix was far greater than regular (87 octane); Solomon's fuel mix was made of the stuff that propels rockets—and his success reached heights never to be reached again.

There has been an overwhelming response to a little prayer by a little-known (until recently) Bible character named Jabez. In Jabez's prayer, you find a number of bold requests for God to bestow blessings on Jabez. And Jabez asked, not for run-of-the-mill blessings, but for great blessings: "blessed indeed." The author Bruce Wilkinson writes that "the power of Jabez's prayer did not come from his boldness and faith . . . but rather it stemmed from his commitment to allow God to choose how he would be blessed, what he would be blessed with, and how his territory would be enlarged." I will go on to add that the power of Jabez's prayer lies within his fuel mix. I am convinced that there are many people who are reciting Jabez's prayer faithfully every day, requesting that their territories be enlarged and that the Lord "bless them indeed" (see 1 Chronicles 4:9–10). However, for a number of them nothing has significantly changed in their lives. Now don't get me wrong. I think they are on the right track by exercising their faith with righteous boldness and intensity.

But **I believe that the windows of heaven are not fully opening up, because their fuel mix is lacking an important ingredient - a God-plan.**

> ***What is fueling your goals, dreams, and aspirations for success? What's the motivation behind the items on your list, and whose purpose will they be serving: yours or God's? Ask yourself why you want success and how the fruit of your success will be used to advance the kingdom of God.***
>
> ***Take a moment and revisit your list. Draw a line from each item to a newly created column where you will write a corresponding God-plan for that item.***

When performing this exercise for the second time, you will notice that some items will naturally come off your list; sometimes one or two things on your list may be holding up the whole package. Second, when making your God-plan for the items on your list, be very realistic and practical. Remember Solomon's proverbial advice that it is better not to ever make a pledge to God than to make a commitment to the Lord and not be able to see it through (Eccles. 5:1–6). For example, if a new home is on your list, it would be unrealistic to make a God-plan to take in every unfortunate person you meet; however, you could let the church know that you are willing to open up your new home as a temporary shelter for a battered mother, a displaced family, or a visiting college student. Last but not least, it is also important to revisit any unfinished business with God, particularly any past pledges or commitments you have not been able to deliver. Sometimes it's hard to get new advances when you still have past-due balances. I cannot advise you how to handle these, because each situation is different. I can tell you, just be open with God, because we are all living proof that God continues to look past our faults and still supplies our needs time and time again.

There is a television commercial for a particular brand of gasoline that demonstrates the benefits of its gasoline and ends by posing a simple question to viewers: "What's in your engine?" I am thoroughly convinced that when it comes to our motivation for success, God is asking us the same thing. Therefore, before replying to God's inquiry, review the seven steps I have outlined on the next page; and most important of all, commit your plans to God's purpose, and they shall succeed. Because it is, after all, the Lord's purpose that shall prevail!

## Seven Steps to Creating a More Excellent Plan

1. Write down why you want success, and list what you want from it.
2. Check your fuel mix by asking this motivation question: how will the items on my list be used to glorify God and advance His kingdom?
3. Make sure your God-plan for each item on your success list is realistic.
4. Commit your plans to the Lord and they will succeed!
5. Revisit and address any unfulfilled pledges, plans, or commitments made to God.
6. Pursue excellence with each blessing God puts in your path.
7. Pray continuously, aim high, focus on the journey, and watch the marvelous works of the Creator along the way!

***What's in your engine?***

## Chapter 4

# Are You Dreaming, or Do You Have a Vision?

Proverbs 13:12 says, "Hope deferred makes the heart sick; but when dreams come true at last, there is life and joy" (TLB). Additionally, Psalms 29:18 says, "Where there is no vision the people perish." I have found, during the short time I have lived in this fast-moving world where time waits for no one, a lot of other things can perish as well! You could replace the word *people* with many other words, and the text would still be applicable—words like *marriage* ("Where there is no vision, the marriage will perish."), *business, family, ministry, church, com-*

*mittee, club,* and *team.* Having a vision is vital to achieving excellence in your endeavors. But what's the difference between a vision and a dream?

At the time of this writing, my mother and father have only known what it's like to be grandparents to boys. My siblings and I have all been blessed with sons; there are no girls (and at this stage in the game me and my siblings are in agreement that my parents have a better chance of seeing Jesus before seeing their first granddaughter). When my nephews were younger, every year during the Christmas holiday, I would take them all out to have some fun and to talk. During one of our outings, while trying to impart some wisdom to them, I said something that I thought was profound, they were less impressed with my words than I was. However, the question that I insisted we discuss was, what do you plan to do when you enter adulthood, and how will you support yourself and your future family?

As the conversation progressed, I heard a lot of lofty replies: one nephew wanted to be a professional athlete, another wanted to be a famous record producer, another wanted to be a pilot, and one wanted to be a surgeon. Finally, after listening to a plethora of these high and lofty professions, in an effort to bring about a reality check without stifling their confidence, I asked them: "Do you know the difference between men and boys?" (This could also be applied to women and girls, but I was dealing with four teenage boys at the time.) I gave them each an opportunity to answer, and as each rattled off his response, each containing some element of merit.

I then proceeded to tell them one of my childhood experiences. I took them back to an old set of concrete steps, affectionately referred to as "the stoop" and usually found on the back of a school, an old house, or an apartment building. I took them back to the time when I was a teenage boy, and how I, along with many of my friends, would sit on the stoop and talk about all of the things we were going to do when we grew up. We would talk about the kind of car we were going to drive, what kind of woman we were going to marry, and, last but not least, what kind of job we would have when we grew up. As time went by, some of us began to graduate from high school, and a few of us went on to enter college. While home on spring break, I would sometimes visit the old neighborhood. If I wanted to catch up with old acquaintances, I would go by the old stoop because many of them were still there, sitting and dreaming about what they were going to do later in life. As more time passed, I would drive by the old stoop and a few of them could still be found there, but now, instead of dreaming about what they were going to be, they talked about what could have been.

I told my nephews that those stoops are filled with a lot of unrealized dreams, goals, and aspirations—unrealized because many of those stoop dreamers became men so late in life that today their dreams are now merely fantasies. For many of them, the question is no longer, what do you want to be? The question is, what dreams can you realistically achieve with the limited life experience you possess at this juncture in your life? Then I looked my nephews in the eyes and told them, "The difference between boys and men is that boys stay on the stoop and dream, but men get off the stoop and work to make their dreams come true."

Proverbs 13:12 describes the effects of unpursued dreams and the rewards of dreams realized in this way: "Hope deferred makes the heart sick; but when dreams come true at last, there is life and joy" (NLT). Webster's dictionary defines a dreamer as "a person who has ideas, schemes, or aspirations that are considered impractical or fantasy." In today's society, we label a dreamer as one who revels in fantasy and as someone whose thoughts and ideas are considered unrealistic improbabilities; yet we label a visionary as one who thinks outside the box, whose thoughts, although seemingly improbable, are classified as revolutionary. I am of the strong opinion that the distinction between a dreamer and a visionary directly correlates to one's capacity to apply wisdom, knowledge, and understanding to the pursuit of one's dreams.

Does that mean that the older we get, the less we should dream? Absolutely not! Please don't miss my point. I am an advocate of dreams and dreamers. Dream big! Dream huge! Dream for things that seem impossible! Dream the kinds of dreams that if God does not get intimately involved, you are destined to come up short. The critical point I did not want my nephews to miss is this: unless you get off the stoop and begin acquiring the wisdom, knowledge, and understanding necessary to make a valiant attempt at making your dreams come true, you will always remain a dreamer and never blossom into a visionary.

Leonardo Da Vinci was a dreamer who became a visionary. Every visionary starts out a dreamer. **The pursuit of the wisdom, knowledge, and understanding necessary to make a valiant attempt at realizing your dreams is what separates the men from the boys — the dreamers from the visionaries.** Leonardo would sit and marvel at birds in flight and dream of a day when a man would be able to fly. However, Leonardo didn't stop there. He began to study birds in flight, documenting their flying patterns and wing movements. He began to acquire the knowledge and understanding that would allow him to make a valiant attempt at developing plans for man's first flight, plans that would contribute greatly to the science of aeronautics, plans that would influence flight as we know it today. Leonardo never saw man in flight, but his pursuit of excellence, his quest to make his dreams come true, and his courage to get off the stoop, transformed him from a dreamer into one of the greatest visionaries of human history.

If you live in a city where the commute routinely tests your capacity to endure pain and suffering, I am sure that while sitting in traffic, you have dreamed about the day when we will have flying cars, just like George Jetson did. These cars would take to the air and fly effortlessly above street level congestion, getting us to our desired destinations in a fraction of the time it takes us today. Now that is a worthy dream, but for me it is merely a stoop dream, a dream I have from time to time as I sit on the stoop—which, in this case, happens to be the front seat of my car. While I was still working on this book, I began working with a client who also had that same dream. I remember talking with him during one of our first meetings, and he began talking to me about his dream of seeing cars fly, unmanned vehicles, planes, and automobiles powered not by pollutants but by the very materials they were made of. Wow—what a dream! But this client, whom I will call Dr. X, was not just a dreamer—he was a visionary.

Dr. X left the stoop a long time ago to gain the wisdom, knowledge, and understanding necessary to make a valiant attempt at making his dreams a reality. As I sat there with Dr. X and listened to him explain his scientific theory and his passion for how his science could be applied to power all kinds of things, my concept of dreamers and visionaries crystallized for me. Dr. X still had the passion and enthusiasm of a child, sharing his great dream of what he wanted to be when he grew up. The big difference between him and a child was that he had acquired the necessary wisdom, knowledge, and understanding to go after his dreams and make them come true. Those who subscribe to a more excellent way (pursuers of excellence) are visionaries, not stoop dreamers.

One of my nephews wants to play in the NFL. For his age, he is a gifted athlete, scoring six touchdowns in a single high school game.

I explained to him that I too had that dream as a child and came closer than many others to making it a reality. But that dream is one of the most difficult things to accomplish when you think about what it takes to make it. It is amazing to me how so many gifted and talented young people dream of playing professional sports yet don't see themselves graduating from high school or attending college. I was fortunate to play for one of the winningest coaches in the history of Pac 10 football. (The Pac 10 conference produces more NFL players than any other conference. Sorry, Big Ten fans!) I played with and against many players who were blessed with an opportunity to play in the NFL, so I did have firsthand knowledge of what kind of athletic ability is required to play at the professional level. I proceeded to ask my nephew who wanted to be a professional athlete if he had done any research on what it takes to get to that level. Then I proceeded to grill him with questions: Do you know how many games you have left before college recruiters make their decisions on their scholarship athletes? Do you know what your forty-yard dash time is and the forty-yard dash times for top college athletes playing your position? What about bench press and vertical jump? Have you contacted any colleges to see what their admissions requirements are? Do you know the names of the coaches of the teams you want to play for, and do they run offenses similar to what you're used to? Do you know how many of their players go on to the NFL, and, most important, how many of them go on to get their college degrees? What extra things are you doing to get better, because *good* doesn't cut it? I could have gone on, but I could see the overload meter in his teenage brain rapidly flashing bright red.

What I was trying to instill in all of them was that the key that starts the transformation process from dreamer to visionary is a plan of action, or action plan. An action plan outlines the steps, processes, and milestones required for getting from the stoop to the stadium, from the stoop to the recording studio, from the stoop to the surgery ward, or from the stoop to the cockpit of an F-18 fighter. **"Where there is no vision the people perish," and where there is no action plan, the dream perishes!** Where there is no action plan, the business will perish, the ministry will stagnate, the marriage will fail, the family will grow distant, and the dream or vision will never become a reality. A good action plan alone doesn't guarantee success, but it does guarantee a greater probability for success. Without one, excellence is merely a dream. Moreover, a good action plan starts the metamorphic process of transforming a dreamer into a visionary.

An action plan allows us to analyze where we are and forces us to take an inventory of our strengths, weaknesses, deficiencies, and, last but definitely not least, our blessings. Someone once said that the key to greatness is understanding one's limitations. A good action plan identifies what we have and what we need in order to realize our vision. It tells us where we are and where we need to get to; but most important of all, it tells us what it will take to get us there!

I am convinced that Christian dreamers should have an advantage when it comes to making great dreams a reality. Christians have a champion, a protagonist, on their dream team. They have a hero who lived, bled, and died so that they could be free to dream—and not just dream, but dream abundantly! **Our personal relationship with Christ empowers us to dream big, because when the gap between our starting point and final destination is as cavernous as the Grand Canyon, Christ gives us something that can build a bridge—faith!** Faith is the substance of things hoped for (dreams), the evidence of things not yet seen (stuff to fill the gaps). Faith, the substance of our childhood dreams, is the evidence that dreamers can be transformed into visionaries.

Martin Luther King Jr. was a dreamer, but it was his relentless pursuit of his dream that transformed him into a visionary. Leonardo da Vinci was a dreamer, but his pursuit of his dreams made him a Renaissance man. Walt Disney was forced to file bankruptcy early in his career because few people believed his dream that animated characters could become as big as real-life movie stars. Alexander Graham Bell had a dream of a device that would one day be in every home and allow people all over the world to communicate in real time, but when he demonstrated his concept of the telephone, the financial world laughed at him. All of these individuals and many others were armed with action plans filled with cavernous gaps. The world laughed in their faces, and they had no idea how the gaps would be filled; however, they had a plan of action and enough faith to pursue their dreams.

The Apostle Paul said "Hope that is seen is not hope at all. Who hopes for what he already has?" (Romans 8:24). If we had everything we needed to make our dreams come true, they would not be dreams, but merely desires or wants. What makes them dreams and visions is the gap that separates our present reality from future possibilities.

One of the great fringe benefits of serving God is that we can hope to fill gaps that seem impossible to fill or too wide to bridge over. Christians should corner the market on *big dreams* because God controls the things that we cannot see and has promised that we will be able to realize things that eyes have not seen, ears have not heard, and minds have not conceived. Christians should never let weaknesses, limitations, or gaps prevent them from developing an action plan to pursue their dreams, even if our dreams seem impossible or insurmountable.

The action plan, even if completed, will not guarantee success, but it does guarantee us the opportunity to achieve excellence. Even with an action plan filled with gaps, we have the ability to excel, to grow, to learn, and to pursue excellence with that with which God has blessed us. And if we consistently pursue excellence, we can accomplish great things because only God can limit how far we go in the pursuit of our dreams. When asked why he didn't abandon his goal for the first electric lightbulb after so many years of failure, Thomas Edison replied, "But those years were not wasted [failures]. I now know numerous ways of how not to make a lightbulb." **True success is accomplished when we can honestly say that we did the best with what God gave us to work with. When we do that, we have gotten off the stoop and started the metamorphosis of moving from dreamer to visionary – moving from boys to men!**

## Chapter 5

# Curiosity Didn't Kill the Cat—Procrastination Did!

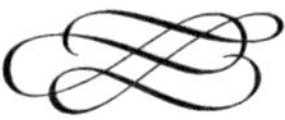

In this book about excellence, I have decided to include a chapter about a murderer. This inhumane creature is a certified killer, a merciless destroyer with an ability to convince people with good intentions to do his dirty work—kill for him! His victims are often unrecognizable, but when they are finally found and unburied, they usually fit this profile: good intentions, personal goals, business objectives, action plans, lifestyle changes, a to-do list, and, last but certainly not least, dreams. This killer won't be found on America's Most Wanted list, but it can be found all over the world. Its name is procrastination.

Now let me first start with a disclaimer so that you don't get a false sense of security. After reading this chapter, you won't be armed with everything you need to overhaul your motivation engine, and neither will you hold in your possession the antidote for procrastination's lethal venom. But what I hope to impart to you is the understanding that procrastination is excellence's public enemy number one. Procrastination will set up a roadblock in your pursuit of excellence and send you on a journey filled with continuous detours, toll roads, and roadblocks that can ultimately cost you your dreams, goals, and aspirations.

I am not qualified to write an entire book on motivation, but I can give you some good experiential insight on the topic. However, I am very qualified to write a trilogy on the topic of procrastination. Now, I am not sure if I was the king of procrastination, but at one time, I was certainly royalty! As a former athlete, the words *plan, focus,* and *execute* have been ingrained into my psyche; yet I still find myself constantly falling prey to the predator—procrastination. It seems that when I make up my mind to begin executing the things on my to-do list or my action plan, I sometimes find myself focusing on things that never seemed important until I started to do something truly important! Procrastination is execution's kryptonite.

Some of the world's greatest debates take place right in our own minds. **Procrastination could be summed up as a war of wills, the battle between our desire to execute and our ability to rationalize, and the power of rationalization is a force of great magnitude.** If you think about it, we all have that force within us because rationalization is a big part of sin's nucleus. Moreover, Christians are the best rationalizers in the world. The reason Christians are such good rationalizers is that we have to be. Our very existence as Christians forces us to rationalize many of our behaviors. Our profession of faith requires us to recognize that we have been called to live by a higher standard; therefore, in order to justify many of our questionable actions, we must rationalize our behavior. Those who live by a different set of principles do not have to rationalize their actions or behaviors as Christians do. The world's standard is public opinion, and the Christian's standard is Christ. The Christian is constantly arguing to convince himself that what he or she wants to do is okay with God. Give me a Christian lawyer every time, because his whole life is a series of arguments before the highest tribunal court known to man and ruled by three supreme justices: God the Father, God the Son, and God the blessed Holy Ghost.

Is procrastination a sin? I don't believe procrastination in and of itself is a sin; however, it is and can be a coconspirator to sin—a sin igniter, a sin instigator. There is no law against the making of sparks; however, people get arrested for arson every day. There is an old saying that "curiosity killed the cat." I beg to differ. I don't think it was the cat's curiosity that did him in. I am sure that as the cat got closer and closer to the edge, or to the top of the tree, or to the middle of the intersection, a still small voice said, "You need to turn around and go back." But the cat most likely responded to the still small voice with words close to these: "Give me a second. I will turn around, but . . ."; "I will start back, but first let me . . ."; "I know I have to get moving, but I need to do this one last thing before I get started." Oo-oo-oo-oh—the infamous *but!*

Procrastination was the spark that ignited the all-consuming fire for the cat, and procrastination is the spark that ignites that which consumes our best-laid plans, our sincere commitments, our resolutions, and our promises. Solomon wrote in Proverbs 6:10, "A little sleep, a little slumber, a little folding of the hands to rest—and poverty will come upon you like a thief and ruin like an armed bandit" (see entire passage of Proverbs 6:6–12). **One of the greatest villainlike characteristics of procrastination is that it causes us to break our covenants with God.** Solomon said when we go before God, it is better to not utter a word (to shut up!) than to make a commitment before God and not keep it (see Ecclesiastes 5:1–6). When we make these commitments, plans, promises and covenants, most of us do so with good and sincere intentions; however, later we somehow find ourselves failing to deliver the goods.

For example, I made a promise to God to write this book for Him after I preached a sermon with this title some time ago. I made the commitment after receiving so much positive feedback from people who told me how much my sermon entitled "A More Excellent Way" had impacted their lives. Recently I ran into one of those individuals, a young, talented professional who has worked for some prominent political figures and is now attending graduate school at a leading university. The young man was in town visiting and said he was hoping to find me at church. He shared how he still listens to the cassette tape of that sermon (the fact that he is listening to it on a cassette should give you an idea of how long I procrastinated in getting this book out) and how it helps him as he pursues his goals in life. I was deeply moved by his remarks; however, when I stopped to think about how long it had been since I first preached that sermon, I was slapped square in my conscience that several years had gone by since I shook parishioners' hands on that day. I could not believe that I had purposed in my mind to write this book so many years ago. I have broken promise after promise and missed numerous personal deadlines time and time again. However, I have been quite productive in other areas of my life. I have completed numerous to-do lists for my stakeholders, achieved many business goals, met many deadlines, and fulfilled many commitments for clients and employers; yet years have gone by and I am still working on this book project.

How is it that we as leaders, achievers, visionaries, goal setters, managers, supervisors, and professionals ask God to put up with the very things we will not accept from our employees, coworkers, church members, subordinates, teammates, classmates, colleagues, children, spouses, and friends? We seem to somehow be able to accomplish those to-do list items that serve our own personal agendas, but when it comes to the things we pledge to do for God and our spiritual growth, we can always find acceptable rationalizations to put them on the back burner, delay the start date, or file them away under the infamous heading "To Be Continued." **I am convinced that our inability to conquer procrastination concerning our spiritual to-do list directly affects our ability to reach our goals and achieve excellence in all other aspects of our lives.**

So how do we combat this goal killer, dream slayer, and vision kidnaper? Here are three rules for fighting procrastination and maximizing our ability to accomplish our goals and achieve excellence.

**Rule #1: We must recognize that procrastination is a coconspirator of sin.**

Procrastination causes us to do the very things that we said we would not do and do not want to do. Paul says that when we find ourselves doing the very things that we pledged we would not do, it is not us doing it, but the sin in us. Oh, the wretched men and women that we are when we allow procrastination to keep us from doing the very things we said we would do, have set our minds to do, or, worst of all, promised God we would do for Him!

**Rule #2: We must recognize procrastination's power over us.**

If we accept rule #1, then rule #2 is a no-brainer. Just like with sin, we cannot beat procrastination alone; we need to evoke a higher power to deal with it. So part B of my second tip is: "Commit your plans to the Lord, and they will succeed." [Proverbs 16:3] If you set out to accomplish something, reach a goal, or attain an objective, no matter how big or how small it is, commit your plans to the Lord and evoke the power of the highest Power— God Himself!

**Rule #3: We must make it a matter of the heart.**

If we are going to gain the victory over procrastination, we will have to make our plans, dreams, goals, objectives, aspirations, and commitments a matter of the heart. I mentioned earlier that I made up my mind to write this book for the Lord shortly after hearing how much my message "A More Excellent Way" touched people. But years went by before I truly acted on that commitment. When I first made the commitment to write the book, I made the commitment in my mind, and I was sincere about making it. Over the years, I did continue working on the project. I made outlines, I named chapters, and I even wrote the introduction and the first chapter. However, up until the day that I ran into that young man, my commitment to write this book, although 100 percent sincere, was still only a matter of the mind. I had not made it a matter of the heart.

Moreover, this was not my first literary project. As a younger man (I am not that old yet!), I had wanted to direct motion pictures. I began working in that industry and even started a business in that industry; I worked on many film projects in various capacities. One summer while away at school, I wrote two full-length screenplays. Two full-length motion-picture screenplays in one summer, and yet there I was, several years after making my commitment to write this book for the Lord, with it still not completed.

Something happened inside me after that young man told me he regularly listens to a tape of my sermon and that it is an important part of how he pursues success and life as a young professional. I thought about his comments and wondered how many people, because of my procrastination, had I left without the chance to be affected. After my encounter with that young professional, I realized I had not made my commitment a matter of the heart—it had been only a matter of the mind. It sounded good to tell others I was working on a book, but I was not working with the passion necessary to make good on my commitment.

I have played and been involved with organized sports for most of my life, but it was a nonsports-related encounter that truly allowed me to understand what coaches mean when they say, "Give me a player with a passion for the game and average athletic ability over a talented athlete with no passion for the game any day." The player with passion will find a way to get the job done, but those who have talent and lack passion easily make excuses, and pass blame when things don't get done.

There is a motion picture entitled *Rudy* about a young man whose passion for the game of football allowed him to fulfill a dream that many gifted and talented athletes never achieve. Even though realistically Rudy would never know what it felt like to stand on the field in the midst of a sell-out crowd and hear the roar of over fifty thousand Fighting Irish football fans, he never stopped pursuing excellence. He had made football a matter of the heart, and he played every down—even though it was only practice—with unbridled passion. And it was that passionate pursuit of excellence that finally allowed Rudy to experience what many talented and gifted athletes dream of: standing on the playing field in front of a sell-out crowd of a nationally televised football game hearing tens of thousands of football fans calling his name.

I remember one year when I was competing for a starting position against an equally talented athlete. The competition was very close, and for the first few games, the coach had me and the other player sharing playing time. We were playing one of the best teams in the country, and the scoreboard was making that plainly clear. We were down by more than four touchdowns when late in the fourth quarter the opposing team fumbled the football. Instinctively I went after that loose ball and recovered the fumble. During the next few games I began noticing that I was not sharing time with the other tackle. One day the head coach came up to me and asked if I knew why I was starting and not sharing the playing time anymore. I told him I wasn't sure, but was grateful. He went on to tell me that while watching the game film, he noticed a player who went after a fumble with great passion at a time in the game when a fumble recovery would not have made a difference, due to fact that our team was down by several touchdowns with little time left in the game. That player was me, I was not starting because of superior athleticism; I was starting because of superior passion for the game.

We all know or have seen passionate people like Rudy in action—people who play every down of life with passion; people who have made their pursuits a matter of the heart; people who pursue excellence on every play, no matter what the scoreboard reads, no matter how much time is left on the clock, no matter what kind of help they have or don't have. They continue in spite of limited resources, talent, gifts, or support from family, friends, colleagues, or teammates. They simply find a way to get it done!

Mel Gibson got it right when he entitled his film depicting Christ's crucifixion *The Passion of the Christ.* At first I did not get it, but after seeing the film, the title crystallized for me. After witnessing a reenactment of what Christ endured for our sake, I am certain that if Christ's commitment for the souls of men, women, boys, and girls had been merely a matter of the mind, He would have never been able to complete His mission. However, because of His unbridled passion to save us from the enemy, Christ died for us while we were yet sinners. **Passion is genuine and uniquely organic. It cannot be bought. It cannot be artificially implanted, inserted, or injected.** Passion must be sown in the heart, and it germinates in the mind, body, and spirit of a man. Find that passion for excellence and live life more abundantly!

## Chapter 6

### Executing the Plan

# Focus, Focus, Focus on Execution, Execution, Execution

While working as a consultant and mentor to many entrepreneurs, I have seen some very good business plans as well as some really poor ones. Yet for every ten businesses that start, six will close their doors within twenty-four months. But it's not just businesses that fail. Six out of ten marriages will end up in divorce. Almost half of all freshmen who enter college will never graduate. Most athletic teams will be under five hundred for the season.

People who start diets will eventually wind up gaining more weight. Churches will never get built, and ministries will stagnate. Projects will be abandoned. Budgets won't be adhered to, and more companies and individuals will file for bankruptcy than ever before. Can one word really be at the root of all this, and if so, what is the word? The one word that serves as the hinge upon which many of the unfortunate realities above swing is *execution.*

*Execution*, as defined by Mr. Webster, is the act of creating, producing, or performing in accordance with an idea, plan, blueprint, order, sentence, contract, or covenant. Again, without a plan of action or some written expectations, goals, or objectives, you are just winging it. You will never have execution without a clear set of objectives. So the first rule of execution is you have to have something that is executable, and that something should, nine times out of ten, be in writing. Unless it (the plan, blueprint, order, sentence, contract, or covenant) is written down, it is still just a concept, an idea, or a thought. Putting it down in black and white moves it from an intangible thing to a tangible, living, executable thing. Recently I stumbled across an old notebook while searching for some research I had compiled for this book. As I flipped through its pages, I stumbled across a list of goals, some business and some personal, that I had written down several years ago. As I ran my finger down the list of goals I realized I had failed to execute many of those things. Moreover, in my desire to better understand why I had failed to achieve those goals, I learned four important lessons about execution. Below are Jim's steps to successful execution.

1. You must put your "execution vision" (I will explain that in a minute) in writing (black and white).
2. You must effectively communicate your execution vision.
3. You must get buy-in (and the team *does* need to buy in to it).
4. You must empower others so they can execute (allocation of the necessary resources to be successful).

Before we go any further, I need to tell you what an execution vision is. An execution vision is more than just your goals and objectives. It goes a step further and adds a visual of the manifestation of your accomplished goals and objectives. An execution vision is what you envision happening once your goals are realized. I think this is a very important characteristic that is missing in many execution paradigms. You can set a goal to accomplish something significant, do what you set out to accomplish, and yet find yourself unfulfilled or dissatisfied with the outcomes of the accomplished goals and objectives. **An execution vision not only lists your goals and objectives, but it also requires you to envision and even list the tangible and intangible desired outcomes, impacts, and results expected from the successful execution of your goals and objectives.**

**Step 1: You must put your execution vision in writing.**

You must make your objectives and goals real and tangible. If I had not put those goals down on paper in black and white, they would have never become real enough to measure. My goals would have been just a distant memory. Truth be told, they were written down, and yet I still forgot them!

However, because I did make them tangible by committing them to paper, I created something real and measurable. In fact, it was so real that several years later after discovering the notebook, I could measure my level of execution as it related to those forgotten objectives. But if I had left it up to my mind to recall my objectives, I would have never realized how ineffective my ability to execute had become. Writing those things down gave me a cold, hard slap of reality. I came to the realization of how fast time moves and how easy it is to lose sight of your objectives if they are not written down and revisited on a consistent basis.

**Step 2: You must effectively communicate your execution vision.**

No man is an island; no man stands alone. There are always other variables involved in order for us to execute properly, and we must effectively communicate the plan of action and the objectives to all the variables in our execution equation. For example, if my goal or objective is to lose fifty pounds over the next twelve months, then I not only have to effectively communicate this goal to myself, but I must also communicate it effectively to all the other variables in this particular execution equation. A potential list of variables in this particular equation might consist of the following: family members, friends, travel contacts, health club manager, personal trainer, lunch partners, coworkers, church members, food list, shopping list, prayer partners, etc. Once I list all the variables in the execution equation, I must then develop an appropriate execution message for each variable. Sometimes we make the mistake of giving a blanket execution message to all of the variables and then fail to execute because the execution message was ineffectively communicated. In the case of losing fifty pounds, I need to do more than just let the family know I want to lose fifty pounds. I need to communicate a message that causes each variable to respond with an action that lends itself to the effective execution of the plan, goal, or objective. Here are a few examples of good execution messages to some of the variables in the equation for losing fifty pounds:

1. Family: "When preparing meals for me, please use these guidelines, because I am trying to lose fifty pounds.": Please use only fat-free dressings on salads. Please do not buy tempting or high-fat foods.
2. Fitness instructor: "Please develop a routine that will allow me to burn more calories and increase my metabolism, because I am trying to lose fifty pounds."
3. Coworkers: "I am trying to lose fifty pounds; therefore, can we go out to eat at a place that has some healthy choices?"

We must learn that it is more than just the communication of the vision; we must effectively communicate an execution message for each variable in the execution equation. Lastly, but certainly not least, every execution message must reinforce the vision or objective. An example of how this would work in an organization is that a specific message would be developed for field employees versus internal staff, managers and supervisors versus line workers, senior staff versus rookies, and young members versus adults. Each group or individual in the execution equation should understand the vision or objective and should clearly know the execution message.

**Step 3: You must get buy-in.**

One of the dominant principles in the book *Execution* by Larry Bossidy and Ram Charan is that execution is the job of the leader. One of many points that I highlighted in the book states, "Only the leader can make execution happen, through his or her deep personal involvement in the substance and even the details of execution." After you communicate the vision objective and deliver the execution message to everyone in the execution equation, your job has really just begun. The next step is to get buy-in; without buy-in, all you have is a message, a messenger, and *zero* execution. It amazes me how a corporation will sometimes try to get buy-in when it needs to cut costs, reduce the workforce, and reduce losses, but then the leaders of the company receive pay increases or bonuses. How much team buy-in do you think that organization accomplished?

Pursuers of excellence lead by example. It is the job of the leader to do more than talk the talk; he or she must also walk the walk. Leaders must not only set and chart the course, but leaders also have to inspect the ship and make sure that all onboard have what they need to do their part so the organization can reach the anticipated destination. And the only way to do that is to take the message personally to all the variables in the execution equation and, what is even more important, demonstrate personal buy-in. It's like the parents who tell their children, "Don't do what I do; do what I say!" Should it be a surprise that parents who drink and smoke but are adamant that their children not drink and smoke raise future drinkers and smokers? No matter what you get out of this chapter, do not miss this: actions still speak louder than words!

I remember during my collegiate days we had successful teams that went to a bowl game every year but never made it to the Rose Bowl. A few years later, my alma mater went to the Rose Bowl three years in a row and won it two out of the three times. Shortly after the Rose Bowl victories, I ran into one of my former teammates who had gone on to a successful NFL career and asked him about the program and what he thought about the great accomplishments of the team (three Rose Bowl appearances in a row). My friend mentioned that he had talked to some of the players from those Rose Bowl teams who were now playing in the NFL, and they told him about a coach he had never heard about. Yes, it was the same coach by name, but the coaching style that these players were talking about was quite different from the one we were used to while playing there.

When we were a part of the program, our coach had one of those infamous coaching towers. This was a high birdhouselike structure two to three stories high. We would see the coach in pregame meetings and Friday meetings, and he would address us after each practice with some final thoughts; but he coached all practices from the tower. To my knowledge, very few players had any kind of personal relationship with the coach. Every season and each game week, he would clearly state the vision or objective, but it was left up to the position coaches to instill it into the team. However, the coach that we heard about from those Rose Bowl and now NFL players was quite different. We heard about a coach who spent a lot more time on the field with the players and who had removed the tower altogether. We heard about a coach who got to know many of the players personally and who communicated the vision and objectives face-to-face, up close and personal. I can't say unequivocally that was the sole reason for the three trips to the Rose Bowl, but what I can tell you is that it was definitely instrumental in getting real buy-in from the team.

**If you want real execution, you have to get out of the tower and get down on the field where execution occurs!** Christ came down from one of the greatest towers known to man (heaven) and came to field level (earth) to ensure that heaven's execution vision was clearly communicated and understood by the whole team.

**Step 4: You must empower others so they can execute.**

After Jesus built His team of disciples, communicated the execution vision, reinforced it with execution messages, and achieved ultimate team buy- in by making the ultimate sacrifice for the team at Calvery, there was still one more important step required to achieve effective execution. After His resurrection, Christ made sure the most important step in the process was done: He delegated and gave the team access to the resources they needed to successfully execute the plan. God empowered them with the tools and resources of heaven and endowed them with the Holy Spirit.

Many times execution fails because leaders fail to implement this final important step. They may implement all the other steps to perfection, but unless they empower the team and give them access to the resources they need in order to execute, everything else will have been done in vain. In some situations, this step may be as simple as giving people on the team the ability to make decisions on their own. There are times when leaders become so passionate about successfully executing their plans or objectives that they become stumbling blocks to their success. In order to have real execution, we have to learn how to provide true delegation. What I mean by true delegation is giving people the freedom to make decisions on their own, but more important, disciplining yourself to accept that those decisions will be different from the ones you would have made if you were tackling that task.

I once worked under a leader who gave a long speech about how he was not a micromanager, but was results oriented and encouraged creativity. On many occasions, he would delegate responsibility, but when people brought back deliverables, he would basically sit there and rework or reshape the deliverable so that it took on the life form of "the supervisor's approach." There were times when this particular leader rewrote deliverables that would say exactly the same thing; it was just that he wanted them to read according to his personal preference.

Execution in that organization failed because in an environment where true creativity and independent decision making were necessary for the goals and objectives to be executed, the organization ended up with very little. Execution failed in this instance because all there was, was a team of clones in an environment that needed a team of talented professionals bringing their individual creativity and experience to the execution equation. A great example of this rule in action is found when the disciples went out among the people to do the work of the Father as instructed by Christ but then came back to Jesus with a complaint. The complaint was that while they were out in the community ministering to the needs of the people, they encountered another group of individuals claming to be Jesus' disciples. They too were ministering to the needs of the people, but without any authorization or supervision. Christ's reply was, "If they are not against us, then they are for us." Christ was giving an Execution 101 lesson to His disciples; He was letting them know that when it comes to executing the plan, they had to stop "majoring in minors" and stop micro-managing.

Jesus was focused on the important goal or objective: are the needs of the people being met? After all, meeting the needs of people is the goal of ministry. The disciples, however, were focusing on style and presentation and missing the fact that the goals and objectives were being met. Does that mean, then, that we advocate taking shortcuts, sacrificing quality, and overlooking controls, checks, and balances? Absolutely not!

For example, if the goal or objective is for three cars to be driven cross-country, washed, gassed, and delivered to the new owners no later than 2 p.m. on a specified day, we should not expect each driver to take the exact same route, rest at preset times, go to the same car wash, fill the car up with gas at our preferred gas station, and choose to eat at all the places we would stop at along the way. What we should expect is that they will be responsible in their choices along the way, notify us of their progress and any unexpected problems, make sure the car cleaning and gas are up to mutually accepted quality standards, and, last but not least, get the car to its destination before 2 p.m.

Christ gave us the ultimate model of how to gain real execution. Jesus developed His team of disciples, communicated the goal or objective, reinforced it with execution messages, achieved ultimate team buy-in at the cross of Calvary, empowered His disciples with the Holy Spirit at Pentecost, left the day-to-day operations to the team, and set up the ultimate open-door policy through prayer. Today those twelve leaders are responsible for organizational growth unlike anything this world has ever seen. So remember, focus, focus, focus on execution, execution, execution!

## Chapter 7

# Lead, Follow, or Get Out of the Way!

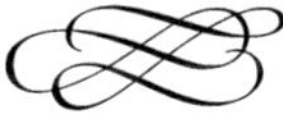

I don't believe one could write a book on excellence and consider it complete without touching on the topic of leadership, for if ever there was a time for exemplary leadership, it is now! The generations that are following many of today's leaders are witnessing a departure from sound leadership principles.

Yes, we still live in a society were we hear the familiar terminology of yesterday's leaders: *teamwork, dedication, recognition, loyalty, hard work, fairness, sacrifice, humility,* and *integrity.* However, the generations guided by today's leaders have witnessed a horrid display of individualism, deception, exorbitance, imposition, knavery, and despotism (now that was a mouthful of adjectives).

Recently I read that the CEO of a major corporation, whose company was forced into bankruptcy resulting from alleged criminal acts committed by senior management, was an active member and supporter of his local church. I dare not deem myself worthy of judging him, but I wonder if he ever looked to Christ for leadership qualities rather than just for saving qualities. Christendom mandates that Christians model themselves after Christ. Jesus said, "Take up your cross and follow me." Therefore, as followers of Christ, we must allow Christ to lead us, not just in church, but everywhere we go. Christians must strive to emulate Christ in their boardrooms, meetings, negotiations, hirings, firings, finances, fiscal reporting, revenue projections, relationships, ministries, schools—everywhere!

Jesus is the Savior for a sin-sick world, but many people miss the fact that Jesus was, and is still, the greatest leader to ever walk the planet.

Jesus and His twelve managers built an enterprise that not even the gates of hell can prevail against! This powerful enterprise (Christendom) continues to grow despite stock- market crashes, world wars, and the rise and fall of political regimes.

The dynamics of sound, solid leadership are applicable in our personal relationships as well as in our business relationships. I believe it does not matter if you are leading a Girl Scouts troop, a Fortune 500 company, a household, a storefront church, or a ten-thousand-member ministry. People want and need to be led; therefore, it is natural for people to seek out and embrace strong leadership.

Children, from their earliest days, look for and crave strong leadership. Children seek out the leaders in their environment, those individuals who are in control of their surroundings. They seek out the individuals who are in charge of things like food, shelter, affection, rewards, and punishment. Children, along with followers of any kind (employees, teammates, members, etc.), instinctively seek to know where the boundaries are and who controls them.

They want to know how things should be done and, most important, who possesses the power and authority to ensure they get done. A child without good leadership will become a menace to himself and society. **And just like a child, an organization without good leadership will also become a menace to itself and society—as we have witnessed with BP, Enron, Tyco, MCI, Lehman Brothers, AIG, and others.**

I was recently at a board meeting where we were discussing the leadership of the organization. One of the board members remarked, "If a person is going to lead this organization, I don't have to like them or necessarily agree with them, but if I am going to follow them, I must respect them." What an interesting dynamic! How is it that you could follow someone you don't like or even agree with? However, many other board members who were strong leaders in their own right confirmed this point of view.

John Maxwell, in his book *The 21 Irrefutable Laws of Leadership,* states, "In general . . . followers are attracted to people who are better leaders than themselves. That is the Law of Respect." How then do you garner that kind of respect?

And even more important for Christians, how did Jesus garner it? When we look to Christ for direction, there are some marvelous principles of leadership we can glean from his 33 years of earthly dwelling. When I think of those who wanted Jesus removed from the scene, they neither liked Him nor agreed with Him, but it was clear they respected Him. There are many dynamics Christ demonstrated that helped to foster the kind of respect required to lead effectively; however, I submit that there are three guiding principles that all of these dynamics fall under. The three principles illustrated by the greatest leader to ever walk the planet (and, for the record, the only one to walk on water) are *conviction, compassion,* and *control.*

| CONVICTION | • Confident<br>• Passionate<br>• Dedicated<br>• Committed<br>• Persistent<br>• Determined<br>• Integrity |
|---|---|

| | |
|---|---|
| COMPASSION | • Fair<br>• Loving<br>• Kind<br>• Concern (Genuine)<br>• Forgiving<br>• Understanding |
| CONTROL | • Firm<br>• Tough<br>• Assertive<br>• Meticulous<br>• Consistent<br>• Orderly |

I call conviction, compassion, and control the "Three Cs of Effective Leadership." Under these three guiding principles, all of the dynamics of effective leadership fall.

The Three Cs table provides a view of many of the dynamics involved in effective leadership and the guiding principle under which they fall. For example, fairness, confidence, and firmness are all dynamics of effective leadership that foster respect; however, each one of these dynamics falls under one of the three Cs. Fairness falls under the C of compassion, confidence falls under the C of conviction, and firmness falls under the C of control.

Respect can be achieved through any of the three Cs, but effective, lasting, and dynamic leadership can occur only when all three Cs are present and active.

Christ consistently demonstrated this model of effective leadership. One of the earliest demonstrations of Christ's leadership ability is seen when He was in the temple speaking with the leaders of the church about the Scriptures. Let's examine this instance and see if we can identify the three Cs in action and the dynamics within them.

First is conviction. It was clear that Christ was convicted of His mission, even as a child. The act of His leaving the side of his parents for several days to perform a task consistent with His mission demonstrated commitment, confidence, and determination (all of which fall under the principle of conviction). When Jesus was discovered by his parents, two days later, and asked why He would cause them such worry, Jesus replied, "Did you not know I would be about my Father's business?" Jesus' reply was assertive and firm, two dynamics of control; however, He delivered it with concern and love, thus illustrating compassion.

When Christ first began His ministry, one of the first things He did, in a subtle yet assertive way, was to establish control. When Jesus recruited the first disciples, He clearly set up the expectations and the role of the relationship they would embark upon together. He said, "Come and follow me"—not "Come and join me," or "Come and assist me," but "Come and *follow* me." Although they would work side by side and often in teams, Jesus made it clear what the chain of command would be. In doing so, He indirectly defined the roles and the expectations of the relationship between leader and followers. Jesus established control within the relationship environment.

**Every relationship environment, whether professional, personal, business, or spiritual, needs to be a controlled environment.** Uncontrolled environments inevitably become chaotic environments. Does that mean we prescribe a tyrannical form of leadership: "I am in control, and no one else is"? Absolutely not! However, it is incumbent upon us as leaders to clearly define the boundary lines within the relationship environment. Establishing control does not mean that we have to do so by dictatorial methods. Control can be established by nonoverbearing actions, but control is vital for lasting and effective leadership. Christ was not overbearing; He was consistent, orderly, assertive, firm, and tough when the situation called for Him to be so. Jesus was always educating His followers about boundaries, but often in the same breath He informed them of the rewards of working effectively within those boundaries.

One of the keys to effective control in a leader-and-follower relationship is that boundaries must be of benefit to both the team and the leader, and these benefits must be clearly communicated and understood. Leaders can lose control of the relationship environment when appropriate control dynamics are not applied. Christ often led with compassion principles rather than control principles, but He never ran from situations that required Him to make tough, firm, and sometimes very unpopular decisions. **Effective leaders must not shy away from opportunities to affirm and reaffirm control principles, just as they should look for every opportunity to apply the principles of compassion and conviction.**

When Jesus saw the abomination going on in his Father's house, He fashioned a scourge, turned over the money-changing tables, and drove the merchants out of the temple. Christ reaffirmed important boundaries and, in doing so, established control and demonstrated conviction. If you always lead with compassion, inevitably a time will come when individuals will challenge boundaries, whether inadvertently or deliberately; and when this happens, you must reestablish control of the relationship environment. Peter, on more than one occasion, crossed relationship boundaries, but his crossings were inadvertent. Christ showed Peter his errors while using control and compassion principles. As a result of Jesus' leadership qualities, Peter was transformed from "quicksand" into "the rock" (a great leader) that Christ would use to build his church. "Upon this rock, I build my church," He said.

I once served under a leader who scored extremely high in the compassion area, but because he was so marginal in demonstrating control principles, the respect level of this particular leader was compromised. A leader who is average in all three categories can be more effective than a leader who is extremely high in one or more categories but absolutely ineffective in another. All three areas must be evident if one is going to achieve dynamic and lasting leadership.

Perception is only half the battle; leaders must also bear fruit in order for their leadership to be effective. Bearing fruit demonstrates credibility. This is where I use creative license and say credibility is the fourth C, but I don't include it in the table because it is a given that a leader must be credible. So, how do leaders bear fruit? The first and most powerful way is to grow it with their own hands, which means to lead by example. Jesus grew His own fruit before He asked others to produce fruit for Him. Jesus demonstrated what man can accomplish through God and what God can accomplish through a man. Jesus demonstrated God's supernatural power for His followers by healing the sick, giving sight to the blind, speaking to the forces of nature—that is, bearing fruit. Then Jesus called on His followers to go out among the people and do the same. His followers went out believing they could bear fruit because their leader led by example. He didn't just say, "Do as I say"; Jesus said, "Do as I do"!

I remember once hiring a young lady for a sales/customer-service position. The young lady embraced the customer-service responsibilities but dreaded the selling aspect of the position. She got to the point were she was ready to walk away from the position because she felt that the selling responsibilities were unattainable for her. One day I told her I would spend some time with her, just observing. While I was sitting and observing her, she reached a prospect that gave her a really hard time. I noticed during her sales pitch that she attempted to speak to prospects in the way she felt comfortable rather than sticking to the script and the selling process (attention, interest, desire, and action). Right after she hung up the phone from that distressing call, I presented her with a challenge. I told her, "If I pick up the phone right now and call that prospect back, and if I get that prospect to respond with the desired action by sticking to the script, would you stay on and try your best each day?" She agreed. I then prepared to call the person back, and as the leader, I knew that it was time for me to bear some fruit for this follower. I was determined not to get off that phone until I produced some fruit. Right after I said a silent prayer in my mind, I called that tough prospect back. After some creative selling, I was able to get the customer to take the action we desired of them.

I saw a complete change in that employee after leading by example and not just serving up lip service. Not only did the CEO of the company take time to sit with her (compassion), but he also led by example, utilizing the same tools the company had been teaching (conviction). I earned her respect that day, and any future instruction she received from management, she now looked at in a different light (credibility).

There is another C worthy of honorable mention that I would add for all leaders, particularly for those who profess to be followers of Christ, and that is character. I have heard some very profound statements about character. A very wise person defined character in this way: ***"The character of an individual can best be measured by looking at the things that individual would do if there was absolutely no way for anyone to find out."*** As leaders, what is at the center of our moral fabric? Are we Christlike in our churches but nothing like Christ in our worldly affairs? Are we like the parents who tell their children, "Do as I say and not as I do"? What are the values and traits not found in our speech but illustrated in our actions? What do we pray no one will find out about us? Christ kept it simple; He said to let your yes be yes and your no be no. James admonished us that a double-minded man is unstable in all his ways.

Leaders are held to a higher standard. Leaders *are* role models, and leaders do not have the luxury of saying, "Do as I say and not as I do." Not every leader will lead in the open view of the public eye or be followed by paparazzi and media; however, every leader will lead in full view of those who follow him or her. Although cameras will not be flashing and microphones may not be thrust into your face at every turn, don't ever believe for a minute that you can lead in a vacuum. Your followers are watching, taking notes, and keeping score.

In conclusion I will simply remind leaders and followers alike that the old adage still holds true: "actions speak louder than words." So lead with conviction, compassion, and maintain control. Furthermore, if you're **not** going to lead, then follow; and if you are not willing to follow, then please get out of the way!

## Chapter 8

# Nothing Beats Failure but a Try

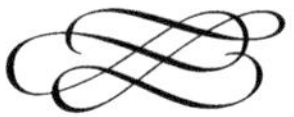

I had an uncle who passed away because of a debilitating disease. I remember visiting with him when he first began showing signs of his illness. My cousin and I were seeking his wisdom regarding a real-estate venture we were considering. (Side note: One of the biggest reasons people fail is from acting on bad advice. Failure to get advice from credible sources will kill the best-laid plans.) My uncle had already retired from public service and had successfully invested in real estate and owned his own business. This was our first attempt at a real-estate investment, so we went to him seeking some advice regarding many of the challenges the deal presented. We discussed a lot of things that evening, but one thing he said to us still rings as clear in my mind today as if I were still sitting there across from him: "Nothing beats failure but a try."

My uncle said that phrase that evening as if that were his trademark slogan. Maybe he had said it to us thousands of times over the years. Maybe he had said it to me on one of the numerous occasions I had spent the night with my cousins at his home, turning rooms in his house into forts, battlefields, tents, caves, and caverns. There were a lot of maybes about the past, but on that evening, those words pierced through my consciousness and plunged directly into my subconscious, and there they have remained ever since. It wasn't long after that evening when I received word that my uncle's unknown illness had finally been correctly identified as Lou Gehrig's disease. And it would not be long before all my uncle's physical assets would be taken from him, reminiscent of a hostile corporate takeover when one day you're in control of all your assets and the next day someone or something has seized full control. It's strange how you may know an individual for many years but have only one profound memory of that individual. In my uncle's case, it was those six words he said to me: "Nothing beats failure but a try."

At the time of the writing of this chapter, I find myself thinking about a young entrepreneur who one day found himself in a heated debate with the individual in the mirror looking back at him. The debate was over those six words, "Nothing beats failure but a try." The man in the mirror had taken the position that there needs to be a limit to the number of failures one should be allowed to experience before throwing in the towel, calling it quits, and playing it safe. But the young entrepreneur standing in front of the mirror was desperately trying to find support for his argument that nothing beats failure but a try.

You see, the man in front of the mirror was holding the broken pieces of a business venture gone bad and now found himself dodging creditors, fighting lawsuits, seeking employment, and staring down at a blank bankruptcy application. The young entrepreneur was ready to give in to the opposition, which was proclaiming that failure is directly correlated with trying so let's eliminate any further chance of failing by playing it safe and taking no more risk. But just when I had resolved within myself to concede the debate (I didn't think you were buying the young entrepreneur story) and throw in the towel, my uncle's words began to echo inside the empty tank that was fueling my spirit: "Nothing beats failure but a try."

However, it was a try that had brought about this present dismal situation, which now had placed me in the midst of a financial storm. It was a try that had brought me face-to-face with a host of hostile financial demons. Therefore, by trying I had brought on failure. At that moment, I desperately needed a deeper understanding of my uncle's words, and I was determined to wrestle with "the man in the mirror" until it became crystal clear.

It was Benjamin Franklin who remarked that there are just two things—that we can be certain of in this life: death and taxes… I submit there is a third and that is failure. However, if it is "a try" that can beat failure then in order to gain a deeper understanding of my uncle's infamous six words ("Nothing beats failure but a try"), we first need to define *a try*.

What is a try? **A try is more than taking a calculated risk. A try is venturing into a realm of no guarantees, no absolutes, and no certainties. Yet, on the other hand, a try is also filled with great promise, great possibilities, and great potential.** A try may be realized in a new relationship, a career change, a business venture, an investment, a diet, a lifestyle change, continuing your education, starting a family, starting a new ministry, building a church, making new friends, witnessing for Christ, and anything else you can think of that requires an investment of some sort with no promise of guaranteed results. But how many failed relationships must we endure before we start playing it safe and stop opening up to people? How many failed business ventures should we pour our blood, sweat, and tears into before we remove *entrepreneur* from our calling cards? How many unsuccessful attempts to build a house of God for the people of God should we agonize over before we put our efforts into something else? And last but not least, how many times should we be rejected in our attempts to witness for Christ before we begin keeping the Good News to ourselves?

When we pursue success in a try, one of the greatest challenges we will face is the fact that we cannot help but measure our progress against others who have tried and succeeded before us. The pursuit of success forces us to measure ourselves through an external looking glass. Looking through an external glass enough times and seeing the spoils of your neighbor's successes against the backdrop of your failures and disappointments can have detrimental effects on your will to try again. When you look outside yourself and measure your success by the successes of others—their successful relationships, their successful business ventures, their successful building projects, their successful evangelistic efforts, etc.—it's hard not to feel like a failure. Actually, it is virtually impossible not to feel like a failure.

When we pursue success rather than excellence, we are setting ourselves up to fail because all of the marbles are riding on us arriving at destinations that have been defined by external motivating factors. When we fail to arrive at these destinations and then compare our accomplishments to our neighbors (the people around us), we run the risk of becoming true failures. **There is a distinct difference between failing at something and being a failure. People become failures only when they get to the place in their lives where they deny themselves the chance to fail at something again.**

When we allow ourselves to be defined by what we have already accomplished rather than by what we can still do through Christ who strengthens us, we give the opposing side's argument a decisive advantage. John Wooden, the legendary Hall of Fame college basketball coach, told his players to never be afraid of failing at something. He went on to say that failures in life are how we grow and that what we should fear more than failing is that we will fail because we did not adequately prepare ourselves to succeed or win. And the only way to adequately prepare oneself to win is to pursue excellence.

God promises a season (life) filled with close games and tough losses, but it's the hard losses and last-second upsets that better prepare us for the difficult parts of our journey. The Word of God makes this crystal clear: "For our light and momentary troubles are achieving for us an eternal glory that far outweighs them all. So we fix our eyes not on what is seen, but on what is unseen. For what is seen is temporary, but what is unseen is eternal" (2 Cor. 4:17–18). If losses and failures prepare us for victory, then some of the greatest winners or most successful people in this life should have a track record of failure. Michael Jordan, who, as one radio announcer so succinctly put it, is unequivocally "the greatest player to ever lace them up" (sneakers or tennis shoes, depending on what part of the country you're from), is the winner he is today because of past failures. His tenacity for excellence and his determination to be the best all-around player to wear an NBA uniform were refined in the Bulls' failed attempts to win an NBA title. To walk away from failure with your head held high is to walk away knowing you did everything in your power to achieve excellence (have you done your best with what God has given you?).

Would Michael Jordan still be the greatest player to ever lace them up if he had never won a championship? **Excellence doesn't show up to make someone great; excellence is a part of someone's greatness! And greatness is a by-product of a lifelong pursuit of excellence.** The world is eager and quick to put people into categories and place labels on them like choker, loser, and failure. It no longer looks at the importance of lessons learned—lessons that build maturity, character, perseverance, patience, and, last but not least, the importance of pursuing a more excellent way. But I have learned that it is not how many times we fail that makes us failures, but rather, it's when we deny ourselves the opportunity to fail that we inevitably become failures.

I spent some time talking with a couple who tried unsuccessfully for nearly ten years to have a child. Despite enduring many disappointments, they continued to try, and in the ninth month of the ninth year of trying, they had their first child. The only way they would have failed to become parents (via natural methods) is to have stopped trying. We don't become failures because we fail repeatedly in going after something; we become failures when we stop trying. A try is a walk of faith, and without faith it is impossible to please God. God is looking for people who are not afraid to exercise their faith, who are not afraid to try in spite of past failures and seemingly insurmountable odds.

Did you know that many of the luxuries surrounding you are the results of repeated failure? How many times do you think Thomas Edison and George Washington Carver failed in creating the lightbulb; Alexander Grahm Bell, in his attempts to invent the telephone; Benjamin Franklin, in his attempts to harness electricity; the Wright brothers, in their struggle to take to the sky; or IBM, in their efforts to build the first PC? Science is predicated upon the notion of proving and studying failure, and some might even argue that science is the study of failure. People often fail to try because of all the pressure society places on us to win and the scarlet letter the world places on those who fail to hit the mark. When we foster these kinds of attitudes ("winning is everything") about success, what we don't realize is that we are creating an atmosphere that fosters failure. When we place so much focus on winning and so little focus on playing the game, we will wind up with two kinds of people: those who want to win so badly that they will do it by any means necessary and those who fear losing so much that they are not willing to risk anything at all.

The latter are the people who play it safe and stay out of the game. They would rather become permanent spectators of the game than risk failing in the game. And when we have a group of people in society like that, we lose out on innovation, diminish creative thinking, stifle growth, and minimize invention. When people feel that failure is not an option and winning is the only thing, we run the risk of stifling the individual with the amazing idea, innovative concept, new paradigm, or insightful theory.

When people see how society treats those who miss the mark, who don't medal or place at the top, it's not hard for them to choose to stay in the stands and remain spectators. For this reason, it is vitally important that our companies, churches, teams, relationships, educational institutions, ministries, businesses, communities, marriages, governments, and, last but certainly not least, our families foster an atmosphere where the pursuit of excellence takes precedence over success and winning at all costs. **When we fail to acknowledge the effort, passion, heart, and desire required to take risk, to reach beyond one's ability, we do future generations a great injustice: we diminish the possibilities of greatness.**

When I look at professional athletics today, I see a profession that has lost its mystique of excellence. One which no longer provides an environment that fosters the creation of great teams and dynasties. Teams whose foundation was the pursuit of excellence and evolved from mediocrity to greatness. What messages are we sending tomorrow's generation when Emmitt Smith, in the same year he breaks Walter Payton's total rushing yardage record, and is crowned the "greatest running back in NFL history," is traded away like a used party favor: "Thanks for the awesome thrills, but we have no use for you anymore"? Where is the lesson for aspiring young minds to achieve excellence, to aspire to be the best they can possibly be, to achieve greatness within the realm of their God-given abilities every time they step onto the field, onto the court, or into a classroom? We are creating an environment that stifles creativity, chokes innovation, and trivializes the lifelong pursuit of excellence. And if we haven't noticed, rest assured - God has!

**Many are waiting for God to send their success to them, special delivery, wrapped in a grandiose miracle, while God is simply waiting for them to get up and try again!** Did you know that Abraham Lincoln lost both times he ran for the US Senate? If we measure success by today's standards, then the American people voted for a loser to serve as the sixteenth president of this great nation we call America. Lincoln, of course, was not a loser. Lincoln was a man who subscribed to God's call for mankind to pursue excellence, and because of it, he went on to become one of history's greatest presidents.

God is calling today's Christians to choose the pursuit of excellence over success. God is still rewarding those who try and fail . . . try and fail . . . try and fail . . . and get back up and try again! God admonishes us to never give up and reminds us that nothing beats failure but a try. In the words of a popular lyricist, "A saint is just a sinner who fell down and got back up again!" For Christians, success cannot be wrapped around the earthly concept of "all or nothing." Christians must seek and identify God's blessings, goodness, and mercies throughout the process.

God has purposed you to succeed at His appointed time—not your intended time. What if Naaman had gone into the Jordan only six times? What if Joshua had stopped marching around Jericho after the fifth time? If Jacob had stopped trying to win Rachel's hand in marriage, there would never have been a Joseph and a tribe of Benjamin. I have learned a lot from my successes, but I have learned even more from the things the world would categorize as failures. When I reflect on those "failure" experiences, there are many things I would have done differently; but if asked if I would erase those difficult moments, those "failures" from my life, I would emphatically say no!

Don't get me wrong. I am no martyr, and I am not advocating the pursuit of failure. However, I have come to realize that failures are important milestones in our lives. These setbacks and disappointments are important footprints in the sands of our lives. They shape us, mold us, and prepare us; but most of all, they make us wiser travelers for roads we have yet to travel. The very things that other people label as failures in our lives are the very things that help us close the gap between what we are and what we are to become!

I think the words of Theodore Roosevelt best personify my uncle's message that nothing beats failure but a try: *"Far better is it to dare mighty things, to win glorious triumphs, even though checkered by failure... than to rank with those poor spirits who neither enjoy nor suffer much, because they live in a gray twilight that knows not victory nor defeat."*

So whatever it is you have attempted to accomplish—that goal or that dream that has eluded your grasp time and time again—just keep trying! The only way out of a batting slump is a base hit, and the only way to get that hit is another "at bat." You have to get back up, stand at the plate, stare down the pitcher, and swing the bat until you make contact with the ball and get to first base. It can't be done from the dugout, and it can't be done from the grandstand. It can only be accomplished at home plate with another try. And when it comes, that hit you have been laboring towards, confirmed by that special *crack* that rings throughout the stadium when bat meets ball at just the perfect juncture in time, all of it (the strikeouts, the hard work, the foul balls, the just misses, the boooooos, the disappointments, the setbacks, (the "failures") will come together, take center stage, line up before you, and take a bow—like a cast of characters playing their parts in one big, God-orchestrated, perfect plan. Nothing beats failure but a try!

**Order Your Extra Copies Today!**

Contact us:

- **for info about booking a More Excellence Seminar or Workshop**
- **to have the author speak at your church or event**
- **for tapes or cd's on "A More Excellent Way"**

**Contact us by e-mail:**

**MoreInfo@MoreExcellence.com**

**www.MoreExcellence.com**

Breinigsville, PA USA
15 October 2010
247442BV00001B/1/P